# BLINK MINI
# USER GUIDE

A Guide On How To Setup Blink Mini
Home Security Indoor Camera, Save
Live View, Placement And Mounting

**By**

**Steven L. Paul**

# TABLE OF CONTENTS

# INTRODUCTION

## A HOME SECURITY CAMERA WITH A STRAP

Everyone loves affordable, good, and super security cameras. Just like the popular Wyze Cam and the entry-level Ring Indoor Cam, the blink mini can be classed among them. It is small and cheap about a $ 35 plug-in camera and able to identify with people's needs when it comes to keeping an eye on their home.

The Blink Mini records in a goal of 1080p empower two-way sound talk from the cell phone application to the camera and can inform your telephone when movement is recognized in one of your designed action zones. It is wide enough to see most of your space because it is about 110 degrees and can even see an object in the dark. If you have other Blink cameras like the current XT2, you can access Mini's clips and all of your other pictures in the same app.

Neither of these features is particularly impressive on their own. At this point, they are expected to come from a smart home security camera, even one as affordable as this one. The Blink Mini meets the standard, but in no way exceeds my expectations. Much of my enthusiasm for the Blink Mini is getting cold because there are other costs involved in getting the most out of it, which wasn't the case with previous Blink cameras.

It will come with free cloud storage through the end of this year. If you already have a Blink account with a previous Blink camera, you will still receive free cloud storage as a benefit. For new users, cloud storage will cost about $ 3 a month per camera beginning on January 1, 2021. With diminishing cloud storage, Mini can notify you when your devices go live. Movement zones and the camera allow you to see a live view from a remote location. However, that's it in terms of functionality. For a device that only does a few things, it hurts to lose some of those features on a paywall.

# CHAPTER ONE

# BLINK MINI REVIEW

## Design

Simple, small, and box-shaped, the Blink Mini sticks to the basics. The front of the camera is black but is in a white cube with rounded corners.

It rests on an adjustable white bracket and comes with two screws that you can use to attach the camera to a wall or ceiling. The design of the Mini is reminiscent of another inexpensive surveillance camera, the Wyze Cam, which is an even more basic white cube that is roughly the same size. They are both small and discreet.

## Blink Mini Rating

Unlike the Blink XT, which runs on two AA batteries and connects to your Wi-Fi network via a small bridge, the Blink Mini connects directly to your Wi-Fi and must be connected. A 6-foot USB cable and a power adapter follow the mini cam.

## Video Quality

You will see that the Blink Mini's 1080p camera offered video that was good but was a little below the quality of the Wyze Cam.

In daylight, the Blink Mini did a fine job considering bright sunlight falls through a window and a lamp in the center of the frame. The colors were bright and accurate, and you can easily see the features of a person as he/she walked into the room. However, one may prefer the Wyze Cam video, which was a bit darker but sharper overall. Both cameras record a 110-degree field of view, which is not as wide as high-end home security cameras but is enough for a device under $ 50.

The nighttime video captured by the Blink Mini was also good for an inexpensive home security camera. He could tell the features of a person quite well while he was in one place. However, faster movements, like someone waving their arms, were blurry.

## App

In the Blink app, you can set a schedule for activating and deactivating the camera, setting the sensitivity, and getting detailed information about the length of the recordings, the recording duration after the movement is stopped, etc.

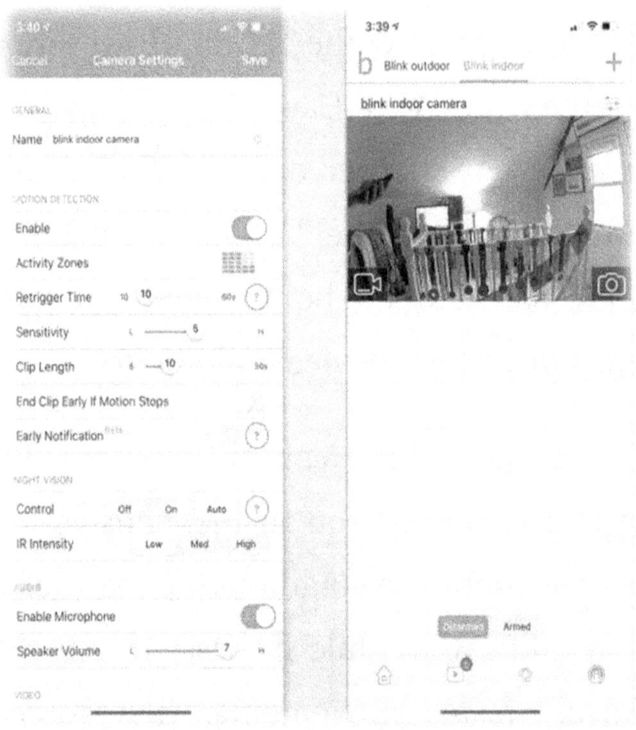

**You can create irregular shapes for motion detection zones:** Blinking shows a still image of what the camera is seeing overlaid with a grid, and you just mark the sections to detect.

**Setting up wyze is simple:** it is possible to create schedules, but a single rectangular shape or square can only be drawn to set a motion detection zone. There are also no settings for the length of a video recorded in the cloud, as Wyze limits the free recordings to 12 seconds. However, the Wyze camera can distinguish between people and other movements (like your dog) so you can only receive notifications when it detects a person.

In comparison to the Wyze app and other indoor security cameras, the Blink app doesn't offer a live view of Mini when the app is opened. Rather, you are shown a static picture of the relatively recent past.

# Video Storage

The camera is built with a free trial of cloud storage subscription till December 31, 2020. If you want to store videos in the cloud after that, a basic subscription costs $ 3 per month per camera and gives you 60 days of continuous storage, But only up to two hours of recording. A subscription to Blink Plus is $ 10 per month. However, you can add an unlimited number of cameras from one location.

With the Blink Sync module 2, which also requires a USB drive (up to 64 GB), you can store videos from up to 10 cameras.

Wyze offers 14 days of free continuous cloud storage. However, the maximum length of a video stored in the cloud is 12 seconds and there is a waiting time of 5 minutes between recordings. If you want to save longer videos and avoid waiting times, you need to save them locally on a microSD card (up to 32 GB, not included). Wyze also offers a paid plan for $ 1.49 per camera per month that records movement in the cloud as long as the movement is detected.

## Smart Home Compatibility

Since Blink is owned by Amazon, it makes sense for the Blink Mini to work with Alexa. You can use your voice to activate and deactivate the camera. If you have an Alexa-enabled smart display (Amazon Echo Show, Echo Show 8, Echo Show 5, or Echo Spot), you can watch a broadcast from the camera on that device. You can also watch a camera stream on your TV if you have a Fire TV device or a Fire TV compatible TV.

The Wyze Cam works with Alexa but is also compatible with the Google Assistant and IFTTT.

## Verdict

While the Blink Mini is an inexpensive home security camera, it doesn't have the value that the Blink XT2 offers. For starters, the Blink Mini costs $ 15 more than the Wyze Cam, which has even better videos as well as additional features like person recognition. If you want to add local storage, the total cost of Blink Mini doubles.

The Blink Mini has highly customizable motion detection, as well as a host of other settings, but for those looking for the best home security camera on a budget, this isn't the best option.

# CHAPTER TWO

# HOW TO SET UP BLINK MINI

Use the instruction below to add your blink camera to an existing or new system.

1.  On the Blink app's home screen, tap the + icon in the upper right corner.

Touch the blue cross

2.  Click the blinking mini camera as shown. You will be taken to the Scan QR

Code screen where your camera can request permission to scan the QR code. This allows you to automatically enter the serial number. Instead, you can enter the number manually. Once the device is recognized, you will need a system.

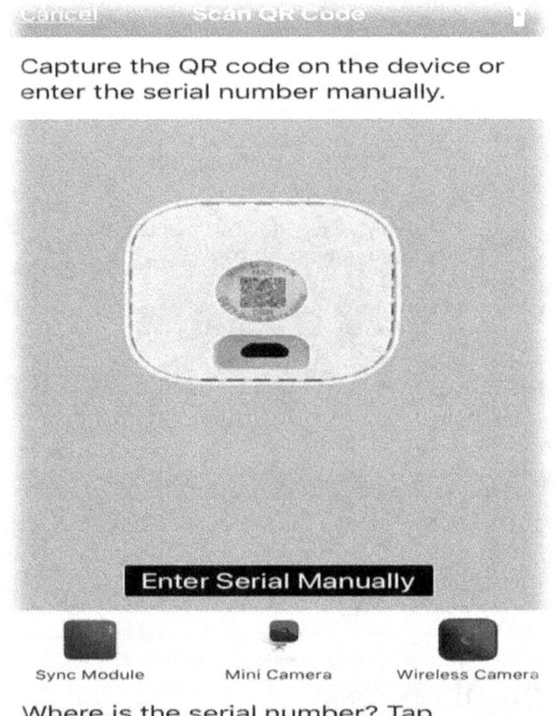

Add a mini to allow the camera to scan the mini QR code on the back

Note:

If your camera doesn't focus the QR code properly, try adding more light to the scene, either with the camera flash or with room lighting.

3. In case you want to add the Mini to a new system, type the name of your system in the text field and it will be created. If you are adding the Mini to an existing system, simply tap the system name to continue.

Choose or click a system name

After selecting next, you will be prompted to connect your camera and wait until one light flashes blue and one light flashes solid green. If so, tap on Detect device, and a connection request will appear: Blinken wants to connect to the network BLINK-XXXX.

Press to find out when the lights on the Mini will flash solid blue and green. Tap Join to connect the camera to Wi-Fi

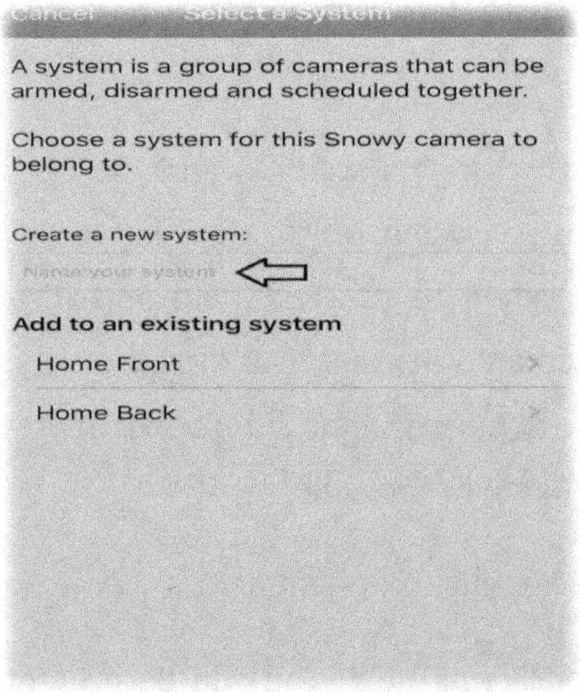


Note: If you don't see the blinking blue light pattern above, you may need to reset the camera. Click here for more information.

4. Touch Join and then choose your Wi-Fi network on the screen that appears. When adding the camera to an existing system, you will need to select the same Wi-Fi network that your other devices are connected to.

When the Blink Servers are ready, the Camera Added screen is displayed. Touch Done to complete the setup and return to the application home screen.

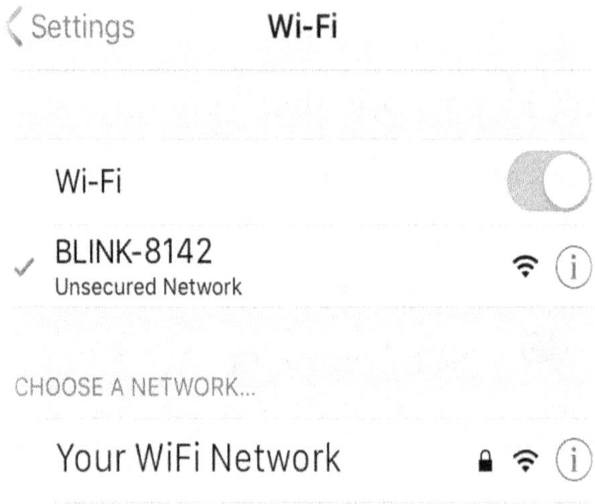

Camera added, tap done

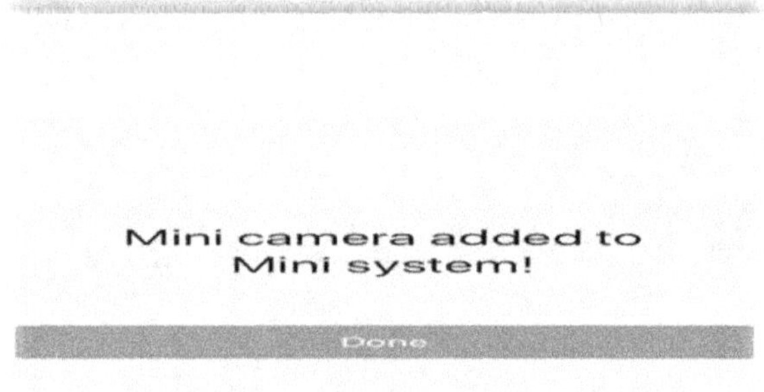

# CHAPTER THREE

# HOW TO SET UP THE BLINK SYSTEM

## Easy DIY Setup

Every Blink system has a synchronization module, which fastens setup and reduces the power consumption of the Blink camera unit. The synchronization module does not require assembly or setup. Just plug it in and follow the Blink app's instructions to get started.

How to configure your Blink system:

1. Plug the synchronization module into a socket
2. Start the Blink app and run the setup wizard
3. Place your Blink unit (s) wherever you want.

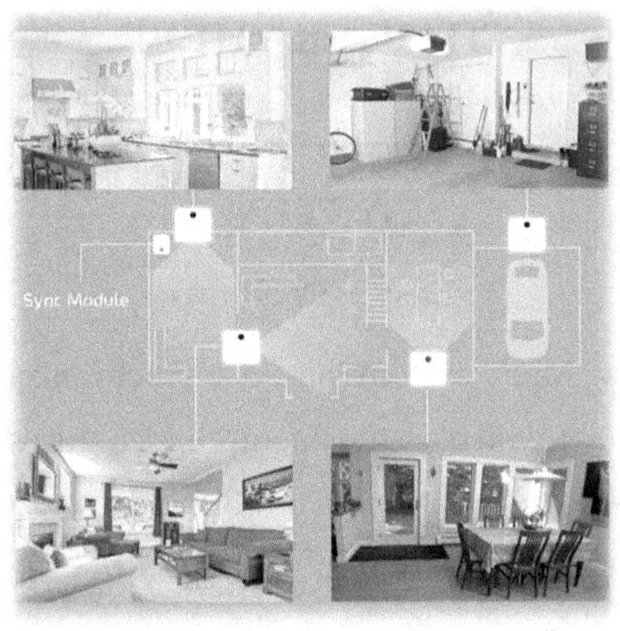


This allows you to create and expand a system that perfectly suits your home. The battery-fueled and remote plan makes it simple to screen all aspects of your home from entryways and windows to the parlor and kitchen, Children's room, or carport.

# CHAPTER FOUR

## SET UP BLINK ON PHONE

To get to your Blink framework from a second or new gadget, you should simply download the Blink application from the significant application store and sign in to the Blink application account with your current email address and secret key.

1. Once you log in, the Blink app will display a PIN entry screen and send a new PIN to the account's email address.
2. Enter the PIN and you will get access.

Since all aspects of their configuration are linked to the account, there will be no reason to create new systems or re-add cameras. Every device that logs into your account sees the same views and settings.

3. To find the account email address on a currently connected device, tap the gear icon in the lower right corner of the screen.

Your email address will be shown at the top of the settings screen that appears.

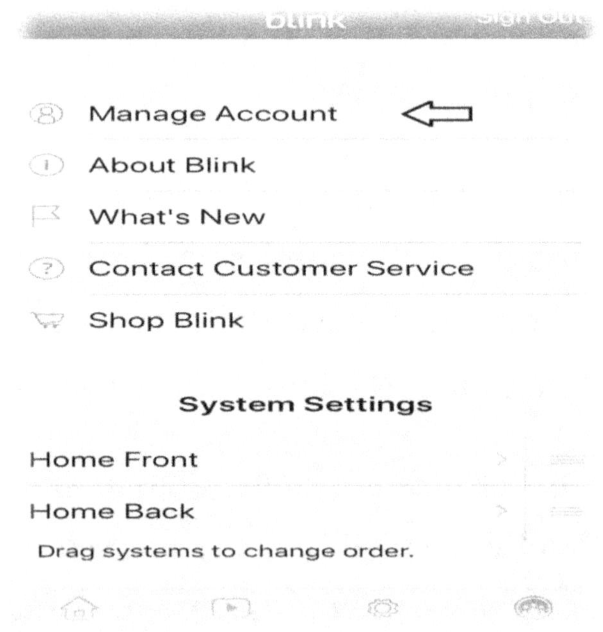


The email address is also displayed at the top of the Manage Account screen.

Email and password information can be changed on this screen.

Account verification starts when you try to change your email address or password.

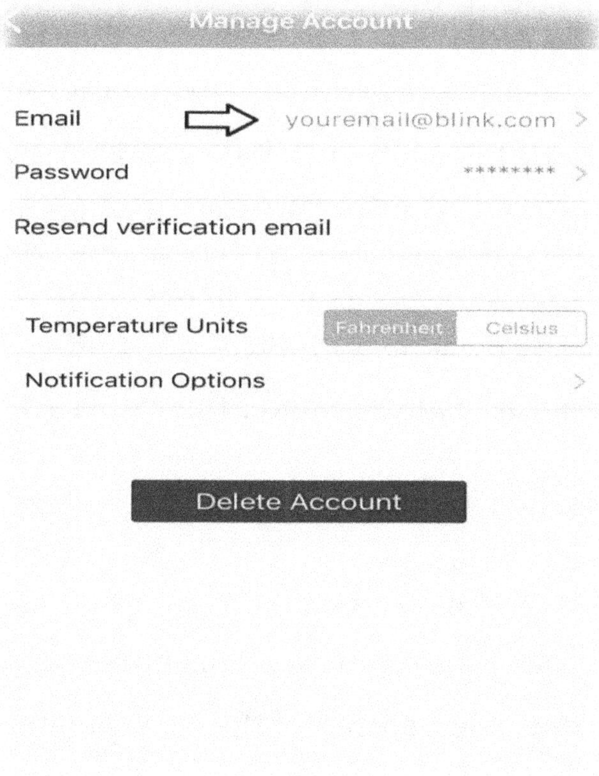

Manage email and password information on the Account screen.

# CHAPTER FIVE

## HOW TO SAVE THE LIVE VIEW ON BLINK CAMERAS

You can record and save your Live View session With the Blink Indoor and Outdoor, XT2, and Mini. Saved live views count towards your 7,200 seconds of cloud storage. So you should know how much space you have and how to delete clips. A subscription is required to save live views for the Blink Indoor (2nd Generation), Outdoor and Mini cameras.

To save live views:

1. First, tap the Live View button on one of your Blink cameras. This button is in the lower-left corner of the camera photo.

2. For one of your Blink cameras, tap the Live View button

3. While using Live View on your camera, you will see the options Save and Discard.

4. Under the video stream, you will see two options. Save and Discard

5. If you tap Save, your current Live View session will be saved and you can discover it on your clip roll with the Live View icon, share it, or save it to your mobile device.

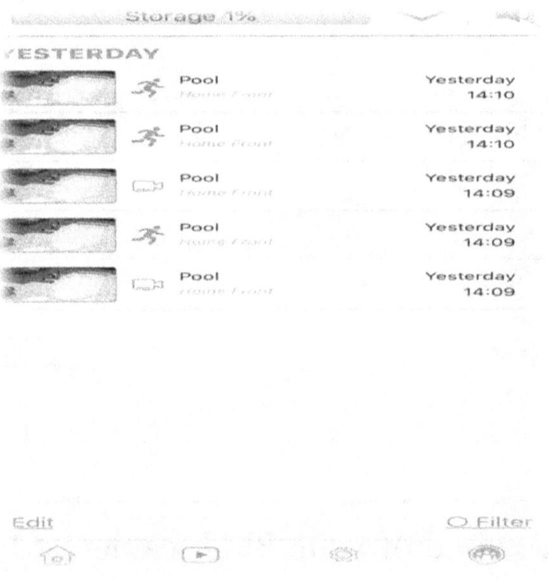

6. Tap on Save. Your current Live View session is saved

Note: you can only edit on iOS devices.

You will find that Live View and saved motion clips each have a different icon on your clip roll to help you distinguish them.

Tap Filters to choose which camera media to display. Alternatively, you can activate the setting to save all live views.

1. To do this, tap the system icon in the lower right corner of the home screen.

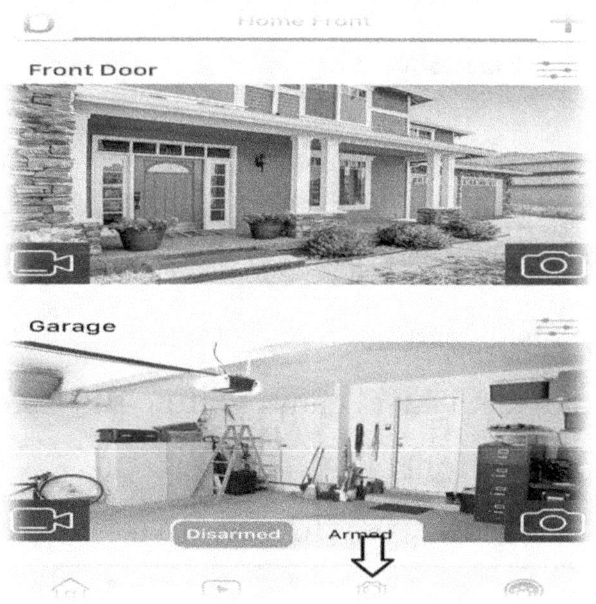



2. Access settings

3. Then select the system in the system
settings below.

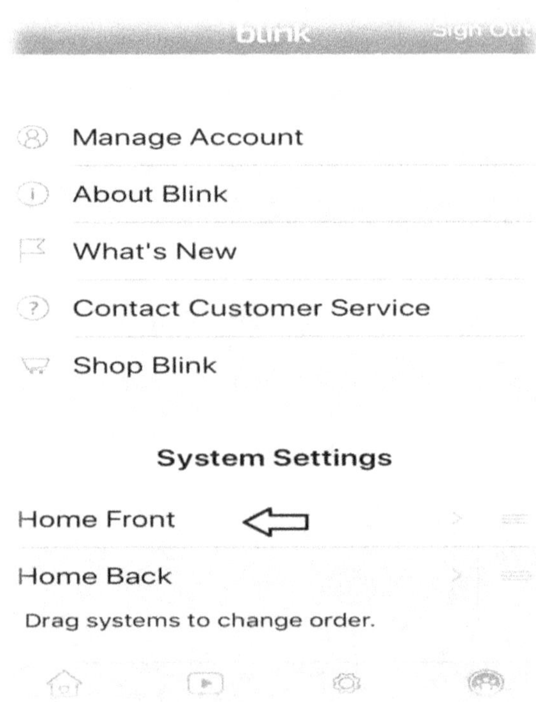


4. Select system

5. Save All Live Views will be displayed at
the bottom of the next screen.

6. Touch the lever to activate this.

Note: If your Blink application is closed before exiting Live View, the clip will be automatically saved.

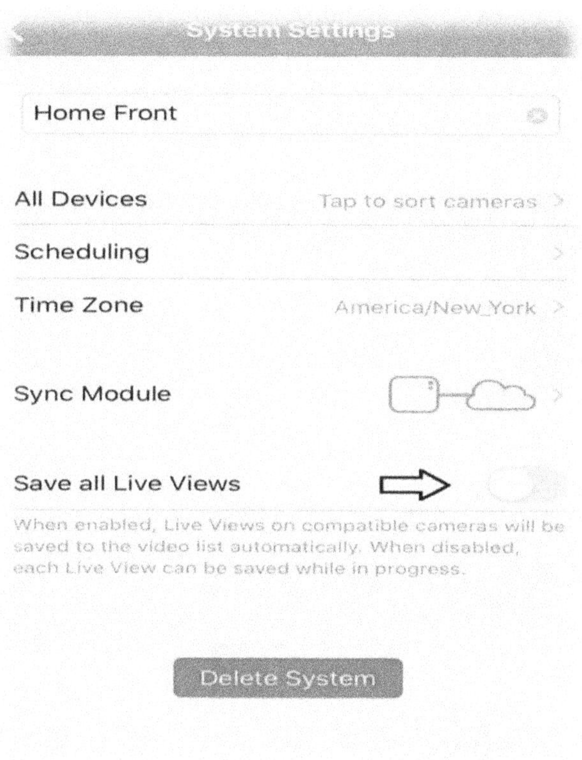



Enable Save All Live Views.

You can record up to five minutes at a time with Live View. This would require the

Continue button to be pressed continuously until this maximum period is reached.

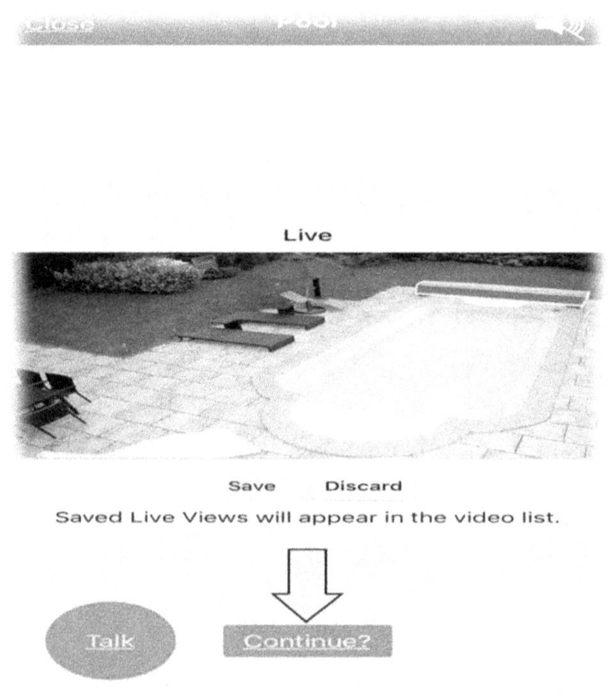


Access settings

If you're using an Echo Show with a Blink camera, you can automatically record live clips of up to five minutes each without having to click next, as Alexa automates this functionality.

You will then need to start a new Live View session.

Blink Mini requires a save option to save live views. For more information on mini storage options, see here. Also, the new synchronization module 2 offers the possibility to save Live Views as clips as long as you have a subscription and use the Clip Backup option.

# CHAPTER SIX

# CAMERA PLACEMENT

Where you put your Blink camera helps you get the images and videos you want.

## Camera View

To observe a location, mount the camera and use the Blink app to test your location with a new thumbnail or by entering Live View.

You can control the night vision functions from the Camera Settings screen. For best results in low light conditions, adjust the brightness of the infrared LED.

## Motion Detection

Whenever anything occurs blink camera alerts you.

To detect motion, the camera is sensitive to the size of an object as it appears in view. Any little creature close to the camera will also trigger the same detection as compared to a larger creature further away since the appearance of its heat signature is closely related. The best detection range is within 5 to 20 feet (1.5 to 6 m) of the camera.

Motion detection is also sensitive to bright flashes such as reflections from cars or sunlight coming through tree branches.

If you want to be alerted to a person arriving on a walkway or path, position the camera so that the direction of travel is moving across the camera's view, rather than toward it. When movement is towards the camera, the image differences from moment to moment are quite small compared to movement moving through the camera view.

To receive alerts about people, rather than animals, you can position the camera so that the view is above the ground high enough that the animal or tail does not activate it.

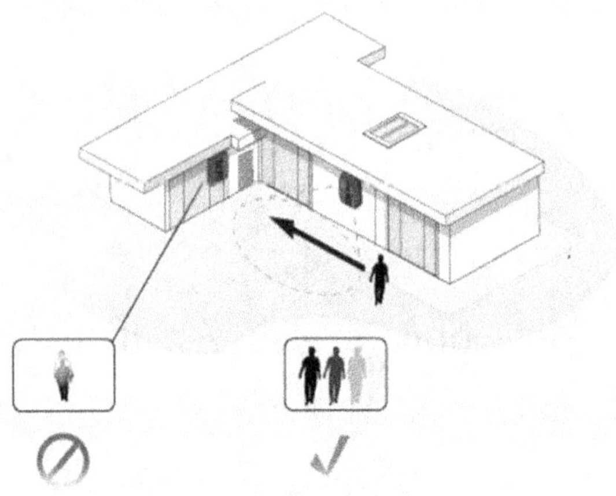

If you are primarily interested in visitors arriving and delivering, it may be helpful to mount the camera facing the door, so that pedestrians or stray animals are not likely to enter the area and trigger a movement alert. Remember that movement across the screen (side-to-side) is more effective for detecting motion than movement approaching the camera.

After setting the motion sensitivity, it is a good idea to test it. Activate motion detection for the camera and activate the system, then walk into view of the camera. Depending on your results, adjust the motion sensitivity settings, change the camera view, or adjust the brightness of the infrared LED. Learn more about how to enable motion detection here.

## False Alerts

In some cases, sources of sudden or large temperature changes can trigger a motion alert. A few guides to consider are the discontinuous enactment of a radiator pilot light, the warmth vent on an outside divider, or an area that is presented to concentrated reflections during specific pieces of the day.

## Image Quality

In general, avoid placing the camera next to a flat surface. Close surfaces can reflect light and form glare and can interfere with the image in various ways. Glare can also be created by momentary reflections or a strong light source directed at the camera lens.

The appearance of the glow can be as fog, a ghost image, or a bright area of the image. The brightness of the glow can also make the background appear darker, as the camera compensates for the additional brightness.

## Activity Zones

Blink cameras can block motion detection in certain areas that you set. Below is an image representing the areas that were blocked to prevent tree movement, its shadow, or blowing leaves from triggering a movement alert.

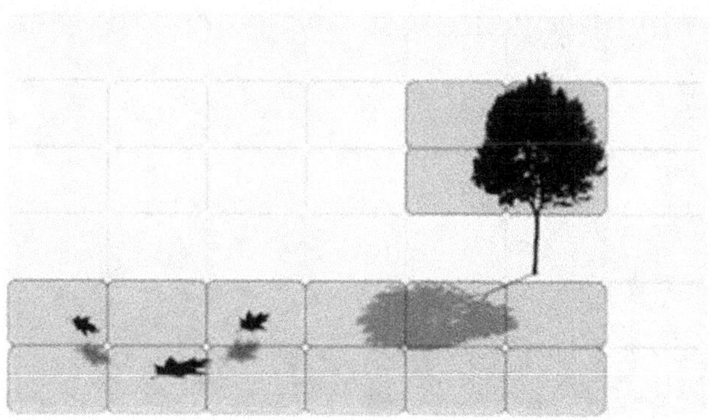

## Camera Positioning

Wherever you place your Blink camera, you will get the pictures and videos you want.

## Camera View

To observe a location, mount the camera and test your location using the Blink app with a new thumbnail or by going to live view.

You can control the night vision functions from the Camera Settings screen. Adjust the brightness of the infrared LED for best results in low light conditions.

# CHAPTER SEVEN

# ASSEMBLING YOUR BLINK XT2 CAMERA

This article will show you how to assemble your new Blink XT2 camera.

When you unbox the Blink XT2, you will see a mounting riser, camera bracket, and two screws. If you want to order more, you can do so at amazon.com.

## Camera Bracket, Vertical Bracket, And Two Screws

A few guides to consider are the discontinuous enactment of a radiator pilot light, the warmth vent on an outside divider, or an area that is presented to concentrated reflections during specific pieces of the day. The two screws provided are wood screws. If you are trying to mount on another surface or masonry work, you should check with your local hardware store for the correct type of screw.

We recommend holding the camera where you want to mount it and testing a live view by clicking this icon in the app. This is a great way to check that the camera has good visibility and signal strength in that location. Better motion detection is gained when an object walks horizontally across the field of view and not directly towards the camera or away from it. It keeps this when choosing a mounting location.

Once you have decided on the location, put the bracket and riser together. (Using the mounting riser is entirely optional.)

### Assemble The Bracket And Riser

You will see that the screw holes line up on these two accessories. Then use the two screws provided to attach the bracket to the desired location. Please note that using the screws provided for the bracket will create two holes in the wall surface.

## The Screw Holes On These Two Accessories Line Up

Once the bracket (and the optional mounting riser) is firmly in place, place the camera on the bracket. The circular part of the bracket connects to the center circle on the back of the XT2 camera.

The circular part of the bracket connects to the center circle on the back of the XT2 camera

After assembly, you can rotate the camera on the bracket yourself to get the perfect viewing angle. When positioning the camera, keep in mind that the best motion detection occurs when a subject crosses the field of view from side to side, rather than driving directly toward or away from the camera.